August 1994

Dear Dan,

Thinking of you — [...]
your garden.

Always remember when you were little and Mr. Anstett and you planted those flowers — how he helped you all summer — only to discover they were weeds! It goes to show you anything can grow if it is taken care of with love!

Love you always
Mom + Dad

ROUND & ROUND
THE GARDEN

To Cairo and Darcy

ROUND & ROUND THE GARDEN

MARIAN FRENCH

Illustrated by Karen Carter

Angus&Robertson
An imprint of HarperCollins*Publishers*

Contents

Introduction

B eauty walks softly in a garden, hand in hand
with tranquillity as gentle as a drift of falling
pollen.

Sense the rhythms of growth and the vibrations
of beauty about us as we languish occasionally in
the shade of our trees to sip tea, or taste a
handful of strawberries gathered moments before.

Forget hostile weather, pesky aphids, bad
backs, ailing chrysanthemums.

Instead, listen to the companionship of birds in
a garden soft from rain. Reach for pleasant things
to touch, velvet soft silver leaves of southernwood
and sage. Bend to the scent of violets and roses,
or turn to capture and inhale a pergola drenched
in a tumble of sweet-smelling jasmine.

Special moments when gardening are most
valued and the world seems far away.

Someone once said, 'A man doesn't know
anything about life unless he puts his hands in the
soil and makes something grow.'

Seasons

A garden as a work of art is not a finished thing like a painting or a sculpture, but chameleon-like it alters with the seasons and the whims of fashion; its compelling charm, the uncertainty.

Spring

In spring the scents of jasmine and honeysuckle fill the air, and a mingling of sights, sounds and scents creates a vibrant urgency in the garden, which brings to life an unaccountable feeling of well being.

I watch butterflies light as thistledown waft amongst the flowers on those early sunny days of spring, seeking the honeyed scent of lavender flowers, sweet alyssum and wallflowers.

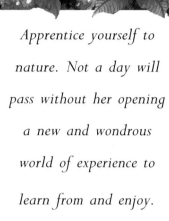

Apprentice yourself to nature. Not a day will pass without her opening a new and wondrous world of experience to learn from and enjoy.

RICHARD LANGER

Little think'st thou, poore flower,
Whom I have watched six or seven dayes
And seene thy birth, and seene what every houre
Gave to thy growth, thee to this height to raise
And now dost laugh and triumph on this bough,
Little thinks't thou
That it will freeze anon, and that I shall
Tomorrow finde thee faine, or not at all.

JOHN DONNE, *THE BLOSSOM*

Summer

• • •

The first rays of the sun bring from the shrubbery and trees outside the incessant shimmering cries of cicadas. Bees swarm in the pulsing heat of the day and forage busily amongst the pale gold flowers of the honeysuckle; while the summer evenings are heavy with the scent of regale lilies, jasmine and lavender.

My delightful Cherokee Rose (*Rosa laevigata*), with flowers as large as teacups, climbs in gay abandon through the white cedar, a backdrop to the clumsy beetles which clatter through the scented evening air.

Autumn

* * *

In Autumn's grasp imprisoned beams
To mystic ardour run,
Each leaf becomes a flaming torch
Lit by the amber sun.

EDNA WALLING

Nature in a last minute fling treats us to a flamboyant burst of colour before Autumn winds dismantle trees of their red, pink and amber gold cover; whispering the end to soft warm lazy days.

As the eager and vibrant growth of spring and summer wanes, there's much to be done, sowing seeds, and planting bulbs for spring flowers, tending lawns and roses, feeding citrus and fruit trees . . . or just pottering.

Winter

✦ ✦ ✦

Even the cold damp garden wrapped in winter has
its own bleak beauty. Sitting in suspended
animation it waits for the first spell of crisp dry
weather to bring it alive with green spikes of
winter bulbs — nodding snowflakes, daffodils and
hyacinth pushing through the cold dark earth; the
promise of spring.

> *Here in this sequester'd close*
> *Bloom the hyacinth and the rose,*
> *Here beside the modest stock*
> *Flaunts the flaring hollyhock;*
> *Here, without a pang, one sees*
> *Ranks, conditions and degrees.*
>
> *All the seasons run their race*
> *In this quiet resting place;*
> *Peach and apricot and fig*
> *Here will ripen and grow big;*
> *Here is store and overplus,*
> *More had not Alcinous.*

HENRY AUSTIN DOBSON,
AT THE SIGN OF THE LYRE, 1885

Colours

How can we not be seduced by colours such as buttercup yellow, rose pink, poppy red, tangerine, salmon glow, bonfire, harvest moon, coral bells, yellow zenith, purple giant, firecracker, lipstick?

Not all gardens depend on an array of flowers for their charm. Some are havens of greenery where ivys pour down in lush profusion from stone walls, and trees provide the shade and dappled light where fuchsias and ferns thrive in hanging baskets, and moss clings to the stones.

As an artiste with a brush, so can a gardener paint his picture and plan his garden, in colours peaceful, joyous to the erotic. Picture a 'pristine garden of white' with a scattering of buffs and apricots . . . or a mingling of all that is pleasant to the eye with a textured 'green on green garden' from the delicate pale to the deepest and glossiest of greens . . . a 'silver garden' with a myriad of velvet soft silver-leafed plants, watched over by roses pinker than watermelon.

By nature I am a spacious gardener, with visions of sweeping tree-filled vistas of country gardens, yearning for coppices of birch trees and cool wooded glades; Edna Walling is my inspiration.

Then again, I see a cottage garden stuffed with a meandering of massed textures, a profusion of colour and fragrance, and I am won, anxious to abandon myself to the infectious informality of it all.

Window box

A ny window can earn a window box. The site
of your window box will partly be dictated
by the size of the long, narrow polystyrene
planters, which make the best liners for the
timber structure. Use 190 x 19 mm (7½ x ¾ in)
dressed oregon. Use simple butt joints at the
corners and glue and nail back and front to edges
and ends. Give the box extra style by painting it
in a smart colour.

How to make a hose picket

This picket will add decorative impact to the corner of your garden bed . . . and protect it from the damage of a corner cutting hose.

For each picket you need a 500 mm (19½ in) length of 50 x 50 mm (2 x 2 in) hardwood, a 200 mm (8 in) length of 15 mm (½ in) copper piping and a turned finial such as those used on the ends of curtain rods.

Here's a delightful idea for a corner of the garden. Gather up or purchase a series of terracotta pots in various sizes, and string them together to make wind chimes. Use thick rope knotted beneath each pot to keep them in place.

Water gardens

The magic of water in a garden is a world within itself.

Prettiest when there is sunlight playing on the surface, where waterlilies flower happily and tiny floating plants and clumps of rushes and reeds thicken and bloom. It will reflect colour and be moved by the wind or tumble over stones or ledges, adding its own gentle sound of music.

Dragonflies will skim and hover dreamily over ponds, against mirrored images of lacy leaves and the sky above. Frogs and tortoises will find their home there.

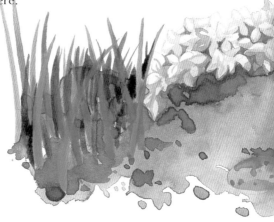

Going to pot

P lanting in containers gives you a portable put-where-you-want garden. As the seasons change and the sun and light alter position, so can the pots be moved to advantage but most of all it provides the instant garden. An immediate solution to soften courtyards and balconies with bright seasonal colour and foliage, filling bare corners and supplying decoration against unadorned walls.

Well-designed containers in quiet neutral shades do not detract from the beauty or effect of foliage or flowers.

Popular in medium to large containers are azaleas, camellias and gardenias for their colourful display from early spring to late summer.

Vines such as ornamental grape and even wisteria are suitable tub plants which will provide cool shade during the hot summer months, then shed their leaves to allow the sun through during winter. They need the support of a small pergola, which will also afford privacy.

Small trees such as myrtle, Japanese maple, pomegranate, all deciduous, give lovely

autumn colour. Cumquat make a neat attractive evergreen tree with the added bonus of fruit, which make delightful marmalade or, perhaps for you, brandied cumquats.

Nasturtiums, impatiens, with colours ranging from dark red through to pink and white, begonias, geraniums and annuals like marigolds, lobelia and alyssum are all suitable for pots or hanging baskets.

A large terracotta bowl makes an ideal mini herb garden. Position it close to the kitchen door and plant sage, thyme, marjoram and other favourite pot herbs; they are nice and handy to harvest when you need them.

In the little garden or courtyard no space need be wasted and there is always something that will grow around and under trees such as orchids, impatiens, coleus, maidenhair ferns, ivy or a ground cover of the little native violet (*Viola hederacea*).

Creatures of the garden

'All morning in the garden I couldn't get myself to go in and write. I come to lunch intoxicated with it all and am told I look like a madman. What have I done to look that way? Merely hunted insects on my rose bushes.'

ANDRE GIDE, JOURNAL 1905

Friends in your garden . . . Dragon Fly which attacks other flying insects.

◆ ◆ ◆

Black spotted Ladybird . . . with capacity to devour 50 aphids a day . . .

◆ ◆ ◆

Gecko . . . eats anything from snails eggs to moths.

'Our earwig traps are not unsightly. We crush sheets of newspaper into fairly tight balls, hide them among the dahlia foliage and overnight the earwigs crawl into the screwed up paper. These are easily disposed of next morning complete with earwigs.'

FROM A GARDEN JOURNAL

I was always the beekeeper in the house-hold, the rest of the family refusing to associate with these little creatures at all: and that was that!

All bees in our garden are referred to as 'your bees', with accusing emphasis uttered in times of painful contact. You see, 'my bees', as with all bees, live by strict social rules. Any interference to this busy and detailed pattern would understandably suffer.

Enter one 'dedicated lawn cutter' accompanied by his motor mower, petrol fumes and noise! The bees' ability to deal with these irritations was swift and direct, culminating in the familiar phrase, 'It's those wretched bees of yours again' as the head of

the family bursts through the
door headed for the
cupboard in search of the
anti-sting.

However, left to themselves,
bees, butterflies and moths all play their vital role
in the life of our gardens, fertilising the plants,
adding delightful colour and interest amongst the
flowers as they collect pollen and nectar.

Did you know that bees can memorise the
shape, colour and scent of flowers, as well as
having a sense of direction, while moths and
butterflies respond more to scent?

Drifts of coloured and scented flowers will
always attract insects to your garden. Beetles and
flies which have short tongues generally visit
wide, flat flowers. Bees and wasps have longer
tongues and can reach inside most flowers but not
thin, bell-shaped ones. Only butterflies and moths
have tongues long enough to get the nectar from
these.

Blue Triangles, Painted Ladies,
Chequered Swallowtails, Tailed
Emperors are just some of the butterflies I see in my mid-summer garden. For
hours they fly and flirt in pairs over a background
of colours from the flower beds regardless of my
presence or that of my Oriental, Darcy.

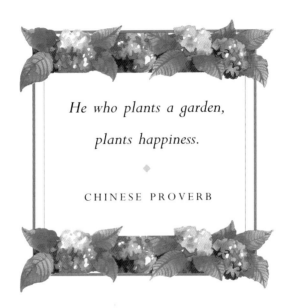

He who plants a garden,

plants happiness.

CHINESE PROVERB

Now Darcy is one creature I had not intended to include in this chapter. However, it's impossible to talk about gardens without this little triangular face popping into the picture. His name I know does not quite fit the aristocrat he is as the Egyptian pharaoh's cat. However, he arrived as Darcy and there it stays. From the first day he joined the household here at Beach Farm, Darcy assigned himself resident keeper of the flower beds. Give him butterflies against a blue sky, add flowers and their perfumes, and the odd catnap to soothe the feline brow and he will explore life at flower-bed level all day long. He sits amongst the flowers gazing at the movement about him, tempted occasionally to breach his good manners and swat the air in a bid to catch a butterfly or moth as they dip and float about him like balloons on a string.

Birds and other friends

I am happiest when I am working in the peaceful isolation of my garden and marvel at the intricacies of nature, pausing to watch frogs and blue tongue lizards demolish my vast slug and snail population. Unashamedly I watch as tiny skinks quick as lightning catch and devour a struggling wayward moth.

Where there are trees there will always be birds. A large English oak dominates one corner of my garden along with liquidambar, jacaranda and native eucalypt. I delight in the numerous birds attracted to the shade of these trees and observe them from my kitchen window as they drink and bathe from the bird bath below. The early days of spring bring a yearly visitor. A watchful, white browed and tail-wagging Willy Wagtail. A constant companion; never still, much less silent, always alert and busy, impatiently waiting for the insects I disturb as I garden. Born opportunists!

Birds are co-owners of our gardens, a partnership rewarded by beauty and song. To encourage their continued occupancy, providing food, shelter and water is but a small courtesy extended to good partners.

To make a simple bird feeder to hang from tree or pergola you need a square of timber about 35 cm (13½ in). Drill holes in each corner. Thread two even lengths of rope through the holes and knot underneath to hold the rope in place. Hang on a hook and adjust the height to suit.

Treasures of topiary

'One man's cherub is another man's gnome'

◆ ◆ ◆

'It is the nature of mankind to change the world about him. Gardeners are perhaps the most practised in this realm.'

◆ ◆ ◆

Ever since 'the Lord took man and put him in the Garden of Eden to dress it and keep it' — Genesis 2

Topiary is a fitting example of the way gardeners have clipped and trimmed box, yew, juniper, privet and shrubbery to

'dress the garden', here human interference is so charming.

The Romans were among the first to indulge their artistic fancies in this way, and it is perhaps to them that we owe the presence of box (*Buxus*) in our landscape. The 'modern' re-emergence of the art took place in the sixteenth century, when the knot garden came into fashion.

Topiary took many forms, with enthusiasts creating mazes in their gardens. The oldest and possibly best known example of this is at Hampton Court, England, which dates from 1690.

In my early childhood topiary was a source of endless enjoyment for me. Animal shapes were popular, with anything from cats to giraffes adorning parks, hedges, and even railway platforms. The fanciful shapes glimpsed

from a train window as we sped by on our rare trips to the city were for me captivating, a continuous parade of fantasy now long gone. The delight of these topiary creations lies in the fact that you can never find two objects that are identical.

Producing topiary is a timely task. Using subjects such as bay tree (*Lauris nobilis*), *Buxus* varieties and *Ficus* can take ten or more years before they are mature pot specimens, however, even in the smallest garden simple topiary will give a 'final touch' and is well worth the effort.

Common ivy (*Hederal helix*) is used as a quick and effective method to achieve various shapes. It is often used to form swags and patterns trained along strands of galvanised wire bolted to brick walls and fences.

Topiary in the round can be fashioned into a standard or hung from a chain by making an ivy ball in a few simple steps.

Fill two round wire baskets with moist long-fibred sphagnum moss. Using short lengths of rust-proof wire, join the baskets together to form a sphere. Use your fingers or a stick to push rooted ivy cuttings through the wire frame into the moss with bent hairpins. Position the ivy ball in a terracotta pot on a short or long shaft of natural tree pruning to suit.

Your topiary ball needs regular trimming. It also needs to be kept moist by daily misting and immersing in water and letting it drain as often as you would water any house plant.

Climbers such as *Bougainvillea* sp., *Lonicera* sp., *Hardenbergia*, *Soalanum*, *Jasminoides* and *Thunbergia alata* can be trained to cover a variety of topiary shapes, fashioned simply from chicken wire.

It is easy to train the main stem of a vine or shrub in a spiral, using a centre stake anchored firmly in the pot. The main stem of the plant must be taped firmly to this support stake in a spiral as it grows until it reaches the height you require.

Remove any excess side branching shoots below the top foliage. When well established, remove the stake.

Gather the harvest

A utumn is the time to gather our herbs and flowers to harvest the seeds and plants we have nurtured during the spring and summer. It is time to dry them out for further use.

To dry herbs, tie the stems loosely into small bunches then hang upside down in a warm, dark, well-ventilated position inside away from moisture for one or two weeks until the leaves are crackle dry. Store in labelled and dated airtight glass jars in a cool, dark place.

Avoid light to keep the colour and perfume of

the flowers and leaves. Also, in the
process of drying and storing, avoid contact with
metal. Metal causes a chemical reaction
detrimental to preserving colour and has an
adverse effect on the perfume.

For culinary herbs it is a good idea to hang
them inside a paper bag to prevent dust settling
on them. This method is used also for collecting
seed from flowers. The seed will fall to the
bottom as the flowers dry.

By drying and preserving the abundant summer
garden 'it stands still' and never dies, the fragrant

flowers and herbs living on in their fragile dried form, being used in many ways to 'further delight the senses'.

Garden Pot Pourri

♦ ♦ ♦

*4 cups dried rose and lavender flowers including rose
leaves for colour
4 tspns orris powder mixed with:
1 tspn cinnamon powder
1 tspn of essential oil of your choice*

Mix last three ingredients together and add to dried flowers. Stir well. Place in lidded container and leave several weeks, stirring occasionally. When matured put into a decorative bowl. Dried orange peel, cloves and bay leaves may also be added.

Eau de Cologne mint has a delightful lasting perfume, as does lemon verbena when dried. Try it amongst your pillowslips and sheets in the linen press.

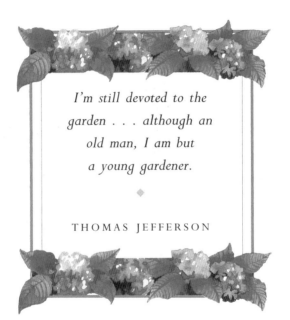

I'm still devoted to the garden . . . although an old man, I am but a young gardener.

THOMAS JEFFERSON

Magic of seed

*'a seed of summer to keep through
winter to plant in spring'*

♦ ♦ ♦

Gardening books can give
immeasurable pleasure to keen amateurs.
The arrival of the latest seed catalogue brings
dreams of luxuriant flowers and delicious things
to eat from one's own garden; visions of what
might be!

The advantages of seed raising are more than
just economic. With seed you have a much wider
choice. There's a real satisfaction in producing
successfully a plant which you have raised yourself
from seed you have also collected.

How to collect and save seed

◆ ◆ ◆

Select your 'specimen' flower carefully. Choose the colour for brightness and a strong-looking plant. Mark this by tying a piece of ribbon on the stem of the bloom you have chosen.

When these have almost died out on the stem, collect and place in an uncovered container (paper bag or glass jar) in a dry, dark place until completely dry. Some flowers may take up to six weeks.

Using a large sheet of white paper or large white plate, open the blooms. Separate the seeds from the dried surrounds (chaff). Place the seeds in waxed envelopes, then seal and label with the species and the date collected.

Joys for children

*'. . . round and round the garden
like a teddy bear . . . '*

♦ ♦ ♦

. . . Remember blowing thistledown from
dandelion clocks to tell the time . . . sitting in a
field of clover on a warm sunny day braiding a
clover chain from the flowers to make a crown
. . . or holding buttercups under your chin
to see if you liked butter or if you had a
boyfriend? The brilliant satin petals
would cast their gold

shadow under our chins, unaccountably settling the point whether or no!

Help children to make dancing dolls from hollyhocks. Show them the hearts in a bleeding heart plant. Teach them how to press flowers and leaves between sheets of blotting paper.

To grow anything from seed is a huge thrill; give them a packet of seed. Let them watch it germinate, potting it on until it is sufficiently mature to plant out; then join the excitement when the first flower unfolds.

Add a little whimsy to the garden by creating a scarecrow. This age-old, not always successful practice for scaring predators from the 'strawberry patch' can be lots of fun.

Stuff a pair of nylon stockings or pantyhose with straw and shape a dancing lady. Add a topknot of straw and hang small mobiles using tin foil so they will glint in the sun as they move and, hopefully, scare the birds away.

Foreign Lands

❖ ❖ ❖

Up into the cherry tree
Who should climb but little me?
I held the trunk with both my hands
And looked abroad on foreign lands.

I saw the next door garden lie,
Adorned with flowers before my eye
And many pleasant places more
That I had never seen before.

❖

ROBERT LOUIS
STEVENSON

Flower cooking

Over five thousand years ago the Chinese made an art of flower cooking, using roots, stems, leaves and petals for decoration and flavour.

Make the most of your nasturtiums; they have ten times as much vitamin C as lettuce. The spicy leaves may be served as a salad or garnished with the flowers. Mix a can of tuna fish with chopped parsley, capers and chives, then blend with home-made mayonnaise. Choose the largest and best leaves and stuff each one with a teaspoon of the mixture. Place carefully in individual dishes and pour over French dressing. Garnish with marigold petals or thyme flowers.

Nasturtium buds, flowers and leaves can be finely minced and whipped into fresh butter.

For a quick snack, use cream cheese, raisins and nuts rolled into a leaf and tied with a long-stemmed flower.

Dandelion: don't underestimate the common dandelion. A maligned weed, dandelions are rich in potassium, calcium salts, manganese, sodium sulphur and the liver-regulating substance choline.

It is an interesting fact that dandelions only live and flourish near human habitation and are to be found all over the world. Every part of the dandelion is edible and the blossom is popular for wine making.

Marigold Biscuits

♦ ♦ ♦

THIS SIMPLE RECIPE IMPARTS A VIBRANCY OF TASTE AND COLOUR TO DELIGHT THE PALATE AND THE EYES. PICK EQUAL QUANTITIES OF YELLOW AND ORANGE PETALS.

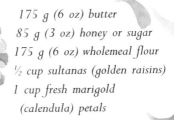

175 g (6 oz) butter
85 g (3 oz) honey or sugar
175 g (6 oz) wholemeal flour
½ cup sultanas (golden raisins)
1 cup fresh marigold
(calendula) petals

Cream butter and honey (or sugar). Add flour and enough cold water to make a kneadable dough. Add petals and sultanas and knead. Roll out, cut into squares or rounds and bake in a hot oven.

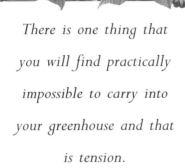

There is one thing that
you will find practically
impossible to carry into
your greenhouse and that
is tension.

❖

CHARLES H. POTTER

Make a delicious drink by adding a handful of
hollyhock leaves to 300 ml (10 fl oz) of wine,
then flavour with ginger and cinnamon.

A rose by any other name . . .

* * *

Elizabethans loved rose petals in their junket, and
Victorians liked rose petal sandwiches for tea.

Sprinkle rose petals on summer drinks and ices.

Dandelion Salad

* * *

$\frac{1}{2}$ cup dandelion flower buds (unopened)
1 bunch young dandelion leaves
2 rashers bacon
2 tblspns apple cider vinegar and oil dressing

Wash flowers and leaves and dry between paper
towels. Fry bacon until crisp, drain. Toss
dandelion flowers into bacon fat and cook until
buds burst open. Crumble bacon into salad bowl.
Add leaves and flowers. Pour on dressing and toss
lightly. Serves 4.

Violet and Watercress Salad

* * *

1 lettuce
1 bunch of watercress
1 large handful of fresh violets
(plus a few leaves)
2 gherkin cucumbers (fresh)
1 tblspn pine nuts

Combine in a salad bowl lettuce
leaves, chopped watercress,
violet blossoms and leaves and finely
sliced cucumber. Dress and sprinkle with
pine nuts.

*The most noteworthy
thing about gardeners is
that they are always
optimistic, always
enterprising, and never
satisfied. They always
look forward to doing
better than they have ever
done before.*

◆

VITA SACKVILLE-WEST

Good neighbours

~

Certain flowers, herbs and vegetables live together in a mutually beneficial way. They help each other by supplying needed nutrients or by warding off insects.

The good neighbour system or companion planting is understanding the interaction between plants and the effects, good or bad, they have on each other. Just like people, some plants just can't seem to get along with certain others. It's not deliberate, just that they need the same nutrients from the soil, or attract the same kind of insect enemies.

Here are just a few tips for better vegies:

chives improve the size of carrots

♦ ♦ ♦

oregano improves the growth and flavour of broccoli

♦ ♦ ♦

basil is a helpful companion to tomatoes

♦ ♦ ♦

borage improves strawberry crops

Plant garlic with tomatoes to guard against red spider, while garlic grown with roses helps to keep aphids away. Grow nasturtiums to combat woolly aphids in the greenhouse and to repel whitefly.

* * *

One plant, the potato, doesn't get along with anyone else in the vegetable patch. He doesn't like anyone to move into his neighbourhood, especially pumpkins, sunflowers and tomatoes. Most members of the cabbage family can't stand strawberries, dislike tomatoes and would rather not live with climbing beans. Beets feel the same about beans so keep them well apart.

* * *

Asparagus doesn't get along well with onions, leeks, or garlic. Beans also have onion problems and carrots don't suffer dill.

* * *

American gardening author Jerry Baker says, 'Potatoes are the Archie Bunkers of the garden plot' — impossible to live with. Also, chives and peas are not on speaking terms at all, and cucumbers are not fans of the folk from the herb family. Corn and celery like everybody.

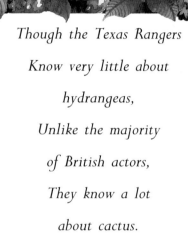

Though the Texas Rangers

Know very little about

hydrangeas,

Unlike the majority

of British actors,

They know a lot

about cactus.

HEATH ROBINSON

Tried and true garden hints

A spray made from garlic is very effective against a wide variety of insects if sprayed on vegetables and flowering plants.

◆ ◆ ◆

Garlic insecticide: 85 grams (3 oz) garlic cloves, sliced, 2 teaspoons paraffin oil. Mix garlic with paraffin oil and leave for 48 hours. Add ½ litre (1 pint) of water and 1 teaspoon of liquid soap detergent. Strain into plastic bottle. Use diluted, 1 teaspoon to ½ litre (1 pint) water.

◆ ◆ ◆

A spray made from wormwood and applied to the ground will help to deter slugs. Pour boiling water over chopped wormwood; stand for 48 hours. Strain and use.

◆ ◆ ◆

Beer is a sure snail bait. Lay a jar containing beer on its side or sink into the level of the soil. They die happy.

Did you know a snail has 135 rows of teeth, each row containing 106 teeth? This means 14,200 teeth per snail each night munching your plants.

❖ ❖ ❖

Mothballs hung in fruit trees will prevent leaf curl.

❖ ❖ ❖

Dripping buried near a climbing rose's roots will help it to thrive.

❖ ❖ ❖

Tea leaves can help stop camellias from dropping their buds.

❖ ❖ ❖

Chives planted beneath apple trees help to prevent apple scab.

❖ ❖ ❖

The brown skins of onions chopped finely and included with the mulch around your roses repels blackspot.

Eggshells also are a good source of magnesium and calcium to be added to mulch or compost.

◆ ◆ ◆

Marigolds make the ideal companion in the vegetable and flower garden. A substance excreted from their roots will kill soil nematodes.

◆ ◆ ◆

Our feline friend can be a problem in the garden. Scatter orange peel on top of the soil to keep them away from your garden beds, as well as mothballs and camphor. Small containers of ammonia dotted about the garden will certainly deter them.

One of the healthiest

ways to gamble is

with a spade and

a packet of garden seeds.

Oddwats

or medieval eccentricities!

~

Garlic sliced and worn in the socks will cure rheumatism.

◆ ◆ ◆

Where rosemary flourishes, the wife rules!

◆ ◆ ◆

The Greeks and Romans believed that people must curse when sowing basil to ensure germination.

◆ ◆ ◆

'Eat sage in May and you'll live for aye.'

◆ ◆ ◆

Parsley is slow to germinate and the magical explanation for this was that before it came up it had to go to the devil and back seven times.

◆ ◆ ◆

Also, a fine harvest was only sure if the seeds were sown on Good Friday, or by a pregnant woman.

~

Tried and true household hints

Parsley sweetens the breath after eating garlic or onions.

◆ ◆ ◆

A sage leaf rubbed on teeth will whiten them and a leaf placed on a mouth ulcer will give relief.

◆ ◆ ◆

Catnip, while pleasing your cat, will also repel ants. Pick fresh and place in ant-infested cupboards.

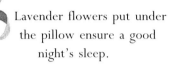

Lavender flowers put under
the pillow ensure a good
night's sleep.

Talk to your plants . . . listen to
what they say. Observe. You can learn
a lot talking to your flowers on a nice
spring morning; spend time in their
company and you will soon be
smiling.

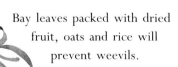

Bay leaves packed with dried
fruit, oats and rice will
prevent weevils.

Gardeners' complaints

Oh, Adam was a gardener, and God who made him sees
That half a proper gardener's work is done upon his
knees.

RUDYARD KIPLING

* * *

What a man needs in gardening is a cast-iron back,
with a hinge.

CHARLES DUDLEY WARNER

In a garden more grows than the gardener sows.

SPANISH PROVERB

◆ ◆ ◆

A garden is a thing of beauty and a job forever.

ANONYMOUS

◆ ◆ ◆

Written on the front of my favourite gardening apron . . .

I dug
I levelled
I weeded
I seeded
I planted
I waited
I weeded
I pleaded
I mulched
I gulched
I watered
I waited
I fumbled
I grumbled
I poked
I hoped
so GROW . . . DAMMIT

Here in a quiet and dusty room they lie,
Faded as crumbled stone or shifting sand,
Forlorn as ashes, shrivelled, scentless, dry
Meadows and gardens running through
my hand.

❖ ❖ ❖

In this brown husk a dale of hawthorn
dreams,
A cedar in this narrow cell is thrust;
It will drink deeply of a century's streams,
These lillies shall make summer on my
dust.

❖ ❖ ❖

Here in their safe and simple house of
death,
Sealed in their shells a million roses leap;
Here I can blow a garden with my
breath,
And in my hand a forest lies asleep.

❖

THE SEED SHOP, MURIEL STUART

Finally, for those who for some reason lack a
'green thumb', don't despair — plant a tree: a
kind old shady oak or maple. Watch it grow and
change with the seasons and in time it will be a
garden of its own: a haven of shade and shelter; a
living testimony to your effort.

Accuse not nature!

She hath done her part;

Do thee but thine.

◆

MILTON, 1608–1674

An Angus & Robertson Publication

Angus&Robertson, an imprint of
HarperCollins*Publishers*
25 Ryde Road, Pymble, Sydney NSW 2073, Australia
31 View Road, Glenfield, Auckland 10, New Zealand

First published in Australia in 1993

Copyright © Marian French
Illustrations by Karen Carter

National Library of Australia
Cataloguing-in-Publication data:

French, Marian.

Round and round the garden: a miscellany of thoughts,
ideas and inspirations for the garden lover.

ISBN 0 207 18050 4.

1. Gardening - Miscellanea. 2. Gardening - Quotations,
maxims, etc.I. Title.

Printed in Hong Kong

5 4 3 2 1 93 94 95